MEMORY

Awakening Dormant Potential

L E A P Learning Empowerment & Achieving Potential

ISBN 978-93-80154-63-3

First published in 2011 by Leadstart
A brand of One Point Six Technologies Private Limited
Unit no. 26, Ground Floor, A1, Shram Safalya,
Wadala Truck Terminal Road, Near Post Office,
Antop Hill, Mumbai -400037.
Email:info@leadstartcorp.com
www.leadstartcorp.com

Marketed & Distributed in India by Unbound Script
2/41, Ansari Road, Darayaganj, Delhi - 110002

EDITORS OF LEADSTART

The Editors of Leadstart are a team of passionate literary enthusiasts with a creative and progressive focus. Our team includes distinguished authors, researchers, contributors, in-house editors, and writing talent from around the world. Many literary projects require a diverse team rather than a single author to write or update the book. These projects often involve cases where the original author is unable to continue, whether because they are unavailable or no longer with us. Our work thus spans a range of content, from original writings to thoughtfully abridged classics, updated editions, and translations

LEAP Learning Empowerment & Achieving Potential

ABOUT THE LEAP SERIES

The LEAP series of books has been conceived as a tool of empowerment for every individual to achieve their full potential.

There are certain aspirations that every person in the world shares. We all want to be happy. We all want to lead fulfilling lives. We all want to find our soulmate. We all want a job we love doing. We all want good friends who will share our joy and sorrow. We all want to believe that there is a purpose to our lives.

While the commonality of these goals spans the globe, their achievement is entirely individual. Each person possesses a unique and mixed gift of strengths and weaknesses, special talents and handicaps. To focus our individual lives on all that is positive within us, all that is possible for us to do, to be and to achieve, we need to take conscious steps towards it. The empowerment of our lives is an individual pursuit. The decisions are yours. The action is yours. To do the very best with what one has been given – that is the ultimate achievement of a life well lived.

You Are You
First, we must recognise ourselves and accept our particular basket of capabilities. Nobody is the same. Nor is it necessary to be like someone else.

Find Your Horizons
Once we are at peace with the composition of our own individuality, we can set out to enhance our capabilities in order to achieve full potential as an individual. We can utilise all the teaching around us to stretch our talents to the fullest extent to achieve worthwhile goals.

Cap The Leak
Once we recognise our potential, we can work to minimise the influence and impact of our weak points to allow the strengths to shine in everything we do.

Row Your Boat
Every day is part of the journey. Sometimes you win the day. Sometimes the day is lost. But you keep rowing towards the shore, towards your goals. In India, it is called sadhana. That special power within you drives you to achieve what you have set yourself to do.

The LEAP series teaches methods of individual empowerment.

ജ്ഞ

CONTENTS

INTRODUCTION

Memory is one of the most extraordinary abilities we possess, a force that shapes our identity, influences our decisions, and guides our understanding of the world. It holds our personal history, our relationships, the lessons we learned through failure, and the moments that made us who we are. Without memory, we would wake up every day as strangers to our own lives. With it, we carry continuity, meaning, and a sense of self that stretches across time.

Yet memory is not simply a mental archive. It is alive, active, and constantly reshaping itself. It guides how we handle challenges, how we learn new skills, how we connect with others, and how we imagine our future. Every thought, every smell, every emotion, every pattern we recognise is tied to countless networks of memory working beneath our awareness. Even the smallest memory, like recalling where you kept your keys or recognising the tune of an old song, reveals a mind capable of organising, storing, and recreating entire worlds of information.

In a time where life moves quickly, and distractions pull at us from every direction, many people feel their memory slipping. They forget names, lose track of conversations, or find themselves repeating tasks without realising it. Students struggle to remember what they studied. Professionals feel overwhelmed by information. Parents juggle endless responsibilities and wonder why simple details seem to vanish. Older adults worry when recall feels slower or less reliable. These concerns are not signs of weakness. They are signals from a mind that is overloaded, under-nourished, or in need of intentional care.

The truth is that memory is not fixed. It does not decline automatically with age, nor does it strengthen only in childhood. Memory is a skill we can train, nourish, refine, and rebuild throughout our entire lives. Scientists now know that the brain can continue growing new neurons even in later adulthood, especially in regions responsible for learning and recall. This means change is possible at every stage. Whether you want to improve your focus, remember names better, recover clarity after stress, support your child's learning, or preserve your mind as you age, the tools exist, and they are accessible.

But improving memory is not just about techniques. It begins with understanding. Memory is shaped by everything we do. Our diet, sleep, movement, emotions, stress levels, hormonal shifts, environment, and daily routines all influence how well we remember. Memory reflects our lifestyle as much as it reflects our biology. When the mind is tired, cluttered, malnourished, or overwhelmed, memory falters. When we nourish the mind with calm, rest, stimulation, connection, and purpose, memory thrives.

This book is designed to guide you through every aspect of memory. You will learn the science of how it works and the experiences that shape it. You will explore the everyday habits that strengthen mental clarity and the hidden factors that drain it. You will understand how children build memory, how adults can reclaim it, and how the brain changes through life transitions like pregnancy, menopause, and ageing. You will learn how to use food, movement, lifestyle shifts, and simple cognitive exercises to train your mind to remember more clearly and more confidently. Most importantly, you will learn how memory is deeply connected to who you are and how you live.

You do not need to become a specialist. You simply need curiosity, willingness, and a small dose of consistency. With even a few changes, your memory can grow sharper, calmer, and more resilient. It can become a partner in your life rather than a source of worry. Every page of this book is aimed at helping you awaken the dormant potential of your mind, not just through techniques but through understanding, awareness, and a renewed relationship with your brain.

Memory is more than recollection. It is the story of your life unfolding moment by moment. And with the right care, it can become one of your greatest strengths.

ജ്ഞ

1

WHAT MEMORY REALLY IS

Memory is often described as the brain's ability to store information, but that definition barely captures its true significance. Memory is the internal architecture of your life. It holds the impressions that shaped your personality, the lessons that formed your beliefs, and the emotions that taught you how to navigate the world. Every experience you have ever lived is filtered through memory, and every choice you make today is influenced by thousands of remembered moments working behind the scenes.

To understand memory is to understand yourself. It is the reason you recognise your home after a long trip and the reason a familiar song can fill you with emotion before a single lyric is heard. It allows you to continue conversations from yesterday, return to unfinished dreams, and make use of knowledge you gained months or years ago. Without memory, learning would be impossible, relationships would collapse, and even basic tasks like dressing, reading, or speaking would lose their structure. Memory is the glue that holds your life together, giving continuity to your identity and coherence to your thoughts.

Most people think of memory as a single thing, something that works or fails. In reality, memory is a collection of different abilities working in harmony. There is the memory that helps you navigate physical space, the memory that stores facts and concepts, the memory that lets you recall feelings or sensations, and the memory that guides your habits without your conscious awareness. These systems are constantly interacting. When you meet someone new, you use recognition memory to remember their face, emotional memory to sense how you feel around them, semantic memory to store their name and background, and working memory to stay present in the conversation. Memory is not a filing cabinet. It is a living network.

This network is shaped not just by information but by attention, emotion, and meaning. The mind remembers what it cares about, what surprises it, and what carries weight. This is why emotionally charged events linger and trivial moments disappear. It is also why memory improves when we find purpose and declines when we drift through life without engagement. The mind needs relevance. When you connect information to your goals or experiences, it becomes easier to remember because the brain has a reason to hold on to it. Memory is both biological and personal. It grows stronger when life feels meaningful.

Modern life does not always support this natural process. We are surrounded by constant stimulation that demands attention but does not reward it with meaning. Notifications interrupt our focus before ideas settle. We skim more than we read. We juggle multiple tasks without fully absorbing any of them. This scattered lifestyle places heavy strain on working memory, the system responsible for holding information in the present. When working memory is overwhelmed, long-term memory suffers. You cannot store what you never truly processed. Many people interpret this as poor memory when the real issue is excessive mental clutter.

At the same time, stress has become a constant companion for many adults and students. Stress hormones interfere with memory formation and retrieval. When the mind is anxious or overloaded, it becomes harder to concentrate, harder to recall, and harder to learn. This is why people often forget information during exams, tense conversations, or high-pressure moments. The brain is trying to protect you from perceived danger, not store information for later. Understanding this connection helps remove the shame people feel about forgetfulness. It is not a moral failure. It is a neurological response.

Memory is also influenced by lifestyle in ways we rarely notice. Nutrition affects the brain's ability to form connections. Sleep strengthens the memories created during the day. Movement increases blood flow to the hippocampus, the region central to memory formation. Even social interaction improves recall by stimulating emotional and linguistic networks. Every part of life is connected to memory, and when one area is neglected, the mind responds. This is why memory cannot be improved through tricks alone. It must be supported by a healthier, intentional way of living.

Children experience memory differently from adults. Their minds are constantly forming new pathways, absorbing information with astonishing speed. This process slows as we age but never fully stops. Older adults may notice slower recall, but the capacity for memory growth remains alive. Neuroplasticity, the brain's ability to reorganise itself, continues throughout life. With the right habits, anyone can strengthen their memory, rebuild weakened pathways, and create new ones. Memory is dynamic, not fixed. Every day offers an opportunity to reshape it.

Understanding what memory truly is restores a sense of possibility. You no longer see it as something you either possess or lose. You begin to see it as something that responds to your choices and environment. You understand why certain things stick, and others slip away. You recognise the importance of presence, emotion, and meaning. You realise that strengthening memory is not just a cognitive process. It is a personal one. The clearer your life becomes, the clearer your memory becomes.

Memory is the doorway to learning, but it is also the doorway to self-awareness. It helps you understand why certain events shaped you, why certain habits formed, and why your mind reacts in familiar patterns. It holds the lessons that carried you through hardship and the joy that reminds you to keep going. When you work with your memory rather than against it, you unlock not only sharper recall but a deeper sense of who you are.

Everything begins with this understanding. Memory is not simply your past. It is the foundation of your future.

ᘓᘐ

2

HOW MEMORY WORKS

To understand how memory works, it helps to imagine the mind not as a machine but as a living landscape. Every experience you have sends a ripple through this landscape. Some ripples fade quickly. Others leave gentle impressions that last for days or weeks. A few carve deep pathways that remain for years, becoming part of the long story of who you are. Memory is not about storing information perfectly. Memory is about creating meaningful connections between moments so that you can build a coherent life. The better you understand how this process works, the easier it becomes to guide it and strengthen it.

Everything begins with attention. If you do not pay attention, the information never enters your memory in the first place. Attention is the gateway through which your experiences must pass before they can become part of your mind. In a world filled with constant distractions, this gateway becomes crowded. Notifications flash on screens. Conversations overlap. Thoughts compete with one another.

When attention is scattered, memory weakens because the brain cannot hold what it barely notices. This is why so many people feel like their memory is getting worse when the truth is that their attention is being pulled in too many directions for the mind to function efficiently.

Once attention captures an experience, the mind begins to process it. This happens in the working memory, a temporary holding space where the brain sorts through information and decides what to keep. Working memory is like a small desk on which you place the items you want to examine closely. It can only hold a few things at a time. When the desk becomes cluttered with thoughts, plans, worries, and tasks, new information has no place to settle. It slips away not because it was forgotten, but because it was never truly anchored. When people say they have poor memory, they are often describing an overloaded working memory rather than a failing long-term memory.

After working memory processes information, the brain must decide whether it is worth storing. This decision is influenced by meaning, emotion, and repetition. The mind keeps what matters and lets go of what does not. If something surprises you, inspires you, frightens you, or moves you, the emotional intensity signals to the brain that the experience is important. Strong emotions make strong memories. This is why a childhood moment from twenty years ago might remain vivid, while a conversation from last week feels blurry. Memory is filtered through what the mind believes is meaningful.

Repetition also strengthens memory. Every time you revisit information, you reinforce the pathway that holds it. This is why practice is powerful for students and professionals alike. The brain grows stronger by returning to ideas over time, building layers of understanding that transform knowledge into familiarity. Without repetition, the mind holds only a shallow impression, and shallow impressions fade. This does not mean you must repeat something endlessly. It means you must revisit it with purpose. A few minutes of meaningful review can accomplish more than hours of distracted repetition.

Once the brain decides to store information, it sends it into long-term memory. Here, memory becomes part of the ongoing structure of your mind. Long-term memory is vast, capable of holding more than you will ever consciously recall. It is organised through associations, linking everything you learn to something else you already know. When you learn a new word, it connects to words you already understand. When you meet someone new, your mind links them to familiar personalities, places, or emotions. The more connections a memory has, the easier it is to retrieve. This is why learning becomes faster when you engage curiosity and experience. The mind thrives on connection.

Retrieval, the act of recalling information, is a delicate process. Memory is not retrieved as a perfect recording but reconstructed from stored impressions. Each time you remember something, the mind rebuilds it using fragments, associations, and context. This reconstruction allows for flexibility, but it also introduces errors and distortions. When two memories blend, you may misremember details. When emotions change, your interpretation of the past can shift. Memory is truthful at its core, but it is not always exact. It reflects not only what happened but how you feel about what happened. Understanding this gentle imperfection helps people forgive themselves for forgetting small details. The mind remembers in a human way, not a mechanical one.

Stress has a profound effect on this entire process. When the body is under stress, the brain shifts resources from memory and learning to survival. The amygdala becomes more active, heightening emotion, while the hippocampus, the structure responsible for memory formation, becomes less efficient. This is why people forget information during high-pressure exams or awkward social situations. Their minds are not failing. Their minds are prioritising safety. When stress becomes chronic, memory suffers because the brain remains in survival mode. Learning becomes harder. Focus becomes scattered. Recall becomes unreliable. Reducing stress is not a luxury. It is a cognitive necessity.

Sleep is another essential pillar of memory. During deep sleep, the brain replays experiences from the day, sorting, organising, and strengthening them. Sleep is where learning becomes permanent. Without adequate rest, the mind struggles to store memories, and the following day becomes foggy. Students often believe studying late into the night improves performance, yet a tired brain cannot preserve what it absorbs. Adults push through exhaustion believing productivity is heroic, but long-term memory weakens when rest is ignored. Sleep is not an interruption to memory formation. It is the heart of it.

Children form memory differently because their brains are still developing. Their emotional memories are stronger, their curiosity primes them to learn quickly, and their ability to absorb language, movement, and social cues is heightened. Teenagers process memories through a more emotionally sensitive lens, influenced by identity formation, peer dynamics, and hormonal changes. Adults rely more on experience and interpretation, while older adults draw on accumulated knowledge but may experience slower retrieval. None of these changes signals decline. They reflect the natural evolution of the mind across life stages.

Technology has reshaped memory in ways we are still learning to understand. We outsource phone numbers, directions, birthdays, and even simple facts to digital tools. While this frees mental space for creativity and reasoning, it also reduces the exercise that strengthens memory. The mind grows stronger through use. When too much is delegated, mental muscles weaken. Yet technology can also enhance learning when used intentionally. Online courses, spaced repetition applications, digital notebooks, and interactive tools support memory by creating structured pathways. Memory thrives not when you avoid technology, but when you use it with awareness.

Understanding how memory works gives you practical insight into your own mind. You begin to see that forgetfulness is often a sign of overload, not inadequacy. You notice that meaningful learning requires emotion, engagement, and repetition. You recognise that lifestyle choices shape mental clarity. You learn that memory is not a fixed talent but a responsive system. It changes as you change. It strengthens when you support it. It declines when you neglect it. It can be rebuilt when it has grown weak.

The more you learn about your memory, the more you learn about your inner world. You become aware of what captures your attention, what you value emotionally, what overwhelms your mind, and what restores it. You recognise that memory is deeply personal, shaped by your personality, habits, relationships, and purpose. Understanding this allows you to approach memory not with frustration, but with compassion. It becomes a partnership between you and your mind. A partnership built on patience, curiosity, and intention.

Memory is not a mysterious ability gifted to a few. It is a living system that responds to how you live. When you understand how it works, you begin to see how much power you truly have.

ᘓᘐ

3

TYPES OF MEMORY AND MODERN CHALLENGES

We often think of memory as a single thing, a single ability that either works or fails based on our age, stress level, or state of mind. But memory is not a single skill. It is a collection of interconnected systems, each responsible for a different kind of mental task. When you understand these systems, you begin to recognise why you can recall childhood scenes with clarity but forget where you placed your keys ten minutes ago. You understand why you might master the concepts of a subject but struggle to remember a list of items you need from the store. Memory is not one process but many, each shaped by attention, time, purpose, and emotional weight.

Short-term memory is the mind's temporary holding space. It holds small pieces of information for only a few seconds, like a phone number you glance at quickly or a sentence someone has just spoken to you. It is fragile, easily disrupted, and limited in capacity. When you feel like you forget something immediately after hearing it, it is usually because your short-term memory was overloaded. This has nothing to do with intelligence or age. It is simply the nature of how the brain handles fleeting information. The modern world places enormous demands on this system. Constant notifications, multitasking, rapid conversations, and digital overload compete for the same small window of mental space, causing information to slip away before it fully forms.

Long-term memory is different. It is spacious, deep, and lasting. It holds the stories of your life, the skills you have learned, the languages you know, the people you love, and the things that shape your identity. It stores knowledge from school, habits from childhood, and insights from countless experiences. Long-term memory grows stronger with repetition, emotion, and meaning. It does not disappear quickly, but retrieval can become slower when stress is high or when distractions interfere with access. Many people fear memory loss when the problem is actually retrieval difficulty caused by overwhelm or fatigue. Long-term memory itself remains robust for much of life, and it thrives on engagement, curiosity, and active use.

Working memory acts like a mental workbench where the mind holds and manipulates information. It is what allows you to solve a problem in your head, organise your thoughts during a conversation, understand a paragraph as you read it, or plan the next step of a task. Working memory is essential for learning, reasoning, decision-making, and creativity. When working memory becomes strained, people feel scattered, disorganised, or mentally foggy. In children, weak working memory often shows up as difficulty following instructions or losing track of steps. In adults, it appears as trouble multitasking, forgetting what you were about to say, or losing focus mid-way through a task.

The digital age puts intense pressure on working memory because it forces us to constantly switch contexts. Every switch drains the mental energy required to hold ideas steady.

Emotional memory is another powerful system, even if it is often overlooked. Emotions act as a binding force in the brain. When something matters deeply, either positively or negatively, the mind stores it with remarkable strength. These memories shape our instincts, perceptions, and reactions. A joyful experience may surface years later and bring warmth, while a difficult event may return with intensity even after time has passed. Emotional memory can guide us wisely, but it can also amplify fears or anxieties. Understanding this helps people approach their emotional experiences with compassion. What feels like irrational fear or stubborn insecurity is often the echo of a past emotional memory trying to protect you.

Procedural memory stores the skills you perform without conscious thought. Riding a bicycle, typing on a keyboard, swimming, driving, and even cutting vegetables are examples. Once learned, these skills become automatic, and they remain stable even when other forms of memory weaken. Procedural memory shows how adaptable the brain is, and it demonstrates that learning is not only about intellect but also about repetition, muscle training, and intuitive practice.

All these memory systems exist simultaneously, supporting one another. Yet modern life challenges them in ways previous generations never imagined. One of the biggest modern obstacles is digital saturation. Our devices hold our schedules, reminders, photos, passwords, contacts, and even our most basic information. Outsourcing memory to technology can be helpful, but it also means we practice less active recall, which weakens memory pathways. When we rely too heavily on reminders, we forget how to remember for ourselves. At the same time, constant exposure to screens fragments attention, which is the first step in forming any memory. Without focused attention, memory cannot take root.

Another challenge is the culture of comparison and perfectionism. The pressure to perform at every age, from school to the workplace, places strain on working memory and emotional resilience. Children absorb more information than any previous generation, yet they are also burdened by overstimulation and academic overload. Adults juggle work, family, finances, social expectations, and digital communication, pushing their mental systems to capacity. Under such pressure, memory becomes inconsistent not because it is weak, but because it is exhausted. The brain is a living organ, not a machine, and it needs gentleness, variety, and rest.

Stress adds another layer of difficulty. When the mind perceives stress, even in subtle forms, it shifts resources to emotional survival. This limits the brain's ability to recall information or store new memories effectively. People often interpret this as personal failure. In truth, it is a biological response. Chronic stress, burnout, grief, emotional trauma, and ongoing pressure all interfere with the natural rhythms of memory. The mind cannot focus, process, or recall clearly when it feels unsafe, overwhelmed, or depleted.

Modern challenges also include the constant consumption of information. Never in history have humans processed so much data daily. News, messages, videos, courses, social updates, and endless streams of content saturate the mind. When everything is consumed but nothing is reflected upon, memory weakens. The mind does not learn simply through exposure. It learns through meaning, context, and thoughtful engagement. Without these, information becomes noise.

Despite these challenges, the brain remains more adaptable than it is fragile. Understanding the different types of memory allows you to work with your mind instead of against it. You learn to create space for ideas to settle. You begin to prioritise quality over quantity. You slow down enough to allow long-term memories to form.

You treat working memory with care by reducing unnecessary multitasking. You learn to regulate emotional experiences so that emotional memory supports growth rather than fear. You become mindful of how technology supports or weakens your mental habits. When you recognise the challenges, you gain the power to navigate them.

Memory is not failing in the modern world. Memory is simply overloaded. When you understand the systems that make up your inner world, you can begin to protect them, strengthen them, and use them more intentionally. Knowledge becomes clarity. Clarity becomes empowerment. And empowerment becomes the first step toward a healthier, more resilient mind.

ജ്ജ

4

THREATS TO A HEALTHY MEMORY

Memory thrives in a mind that feels supported, nourished, rested, and balanced. Yet the world we live in today creates conditions that pull us in the opposite direction. It asks us to multitask constantly, to move quickly, to absorb more information than we can process, and to perform at a pace that the human brain was never meant to sustain. When memory falters, people often blame age or intelligence or assume something is wrong with them. But in reality, memory is often responding to the pressures around it. A healthy memory is not simply a product of biology. It is shaped every day by lifestyle, emotion, habit, bodily changes, and environment. Understanding what threatens it is the first step toward protecting it.

One of the most serious modern threats to memory is lack of sleep. Sleep is not rest in the passive sense. It is the time when the brain organises the events of the day, clears mental waste, and strengthens the pathways that hold important information. Without adequate sleep, these processes cannot take place. People who sleep poorly often describe their minds as foggy or heavy. They may forget conversations, misplace objects, or lose track of what they were thinking a moment ago. Even small lapses like repeating a task, forgetting a route, or completely blanking out during a meeting are signs that the brain is struggling to encode new information. Children and adolescents are especially vulnerable because their brains are still developing, yet they often face demanding schedules and late-night screen exposure that disrupt natural cycles. Sleep is one of the simplest and most powerful protectors of memory, yet it is widely neglected.

Another major threat is constant multitasking. The idea that we can juggle multiple things at once is an illusion. What the brain is actually doing is switching rapidly between tasks, and every switch burns cognitive energy. Working memory, which is responsible for holding and manipulating information, becomes overloaded. This leads to mistakes, forgetfulness, and frustration. Many people experience this as the feeling that they are always busy but never fully present. Information slips away before it has time to settle. In a world where notifications interrupt thoughts and digital devices pull attention in multiple directions, multitasking has become the default mode of living. The brain, however, was built for focused attention, not fractured attention.

Stress adds another layer of difficulty. When the body experiences stress, it releases cortisol, a hormone that prepares the body for survival. In small doses, cortisol can improve focus. But when stress becomes chronic, cortisol suppresses memory formation by weakening the regions that store and retrieve information. People under long-term stress often describe their minds as scattered, jittery, or overloaded. They forget simple things, struggle to recall what they just read, and feel mentally drained even when doing nothing. Emotional stress, whether caused by work pressure, personal conflict, grief, fear, or uncertainty, affects memory just as much as physical strain does. The brain cannot focus clearly when it feels threatened or overwhelmed. Memory is not simply a storage tool. It is deeply tied to emotional safety.

Diet and hydration also influence memory more than most people realise. The brain needs a steady flow of nutrients, healthy fats, antioxidants, and hydration to function properly. When the body is undernourished, the mind becomes sluggish. Highly processed foods, sugar-heavy meals, and excessive caffeine can create sharp rises in energy followed by crashes that leave the brain fatigued and disoriented. Dehydration, even mild, affects focus, concentration, and recall. A person may think they are having a memory problem when the real issue is a lack of fuel and water. Over time, a poor diet contributes to inflammation and oxidative stress, both of which accelerate cognitive decline. The modern diet is abundant in calories but often lacking in brain-supportive nutrients, which makes the mind vulnerable.

Environmental disorganisation is another powerful threat. A cluttered space often leads to a cluttered mind. When your environment is chaotic, the brain has to work harder to locate objects, remember tasks, or switch between activities. This increases cognitive load and makes memory less efficient. Many people find that after cleaning their desk, rearranging their home, or simplifying their digital space, their mind feels clearer. This is not just psychological. It is a direct connection between the external world and internal clarity. Our surroundings influence how easily memory forms and how smoothly information flows.

Medical conditions can also impair memory, ranging from temporary disruptions to long-term decline. Conditions like Alzheimer's disease, dementia, and certain neurological disorders directly affect the areas of the brain responsible for forming new memories. Head injuries can disrupt both short-term and long-term recall. Hormonal changes such as menopause, pregnancy, or male hormonal decline influence memory through shifts in brain chemistry, sleep patterns, and emotional stability. Psychological conditions such as depression, anxiety, and post-traumatic stress create emotional states that interfere with encoding and retrieval. Understanding these biological and emotional factors helps reduce self-blame and encourages people to seek support rather than hiding their struggles.

Trauma is one of the most misunderstood influences on memory. The mind protects itself by suppressing or fragmenting memories that feel too painful to process. This is not a flaw. It is a survival response. People often feel confused when they cannot recall certain details or when memories surface suddenly after years of silence. Trauma shapes memory through emotion, not logic. The brain prioritises safety over clarity. Recognising this softens self-judgment and opens the possibility for healing.

The modern world also exposes the brain to an overload of digital information. Constant scrolling, reading multiple updates, consuming endless videos, and absorbing fragmented content weakens attention. Without attention, memory cannot take root. The mind becomes accustomed to quick shifts rather than deep focus. This leads to a sense of mental fatigue where people feel they cannot retain anything. It is not poor memory. It is an overwhelmed memory system struggling to find space for what truly matters.

Hormonal changes create another layer of complexity. Menopause can cause cognitive fog as estrogen levels shift, affecting brain connectivity. Pregnancy can produce forgetfulness due to hormonal fluctuations, sleep disruption, and emotional transitions. Men experience hormonal changes too, although more gradually. These shifts affect mood, focus, clarity, and mental endurance. The mind reflects the body's internal cycles. When hormones shift, memory responds.

Age itself is not the enemy. While ageing brings natural changes in neuron speed and cognitive flexibility, memory decline is often accelerated by lifestyle rather than age alone. Many older adults remain mentally sharp because they live with structure, engagement, curiosity, movement, and meaningful routine. Memory thrives when used, protected, and nourished.

Recognising these threats is not meant to alarm but to empower. Each factor explains why memory struggles at times, and each factor is also an opportunity for renewal. When you understand what weakens memory, you begin to make choices that support it. You learn to protect your sleep, reduce multitasking, manage stress gently, nourish your mind through nutrition, care for your emotional world, honour your body's rhythms, and create an environment that supports mental clarity. Memory does not weaken because you are incapable. It weakens because the conditions around it demand more than it can carry. With awareness and intention, those conditions can be reshaped.

ꕥ

5

EVERYDAY HABITS THAT STRENGTHEN MEMORY

Memory does not improve through occasional effort. It grows through rhythm, repetition, and gentle consistency. The habits you weave into your days influence not only how clearly you think but also how deeply you engage with the world. People often imagine memory improvement as something complicated or scientific, but in truth, the most powerful tools are simple actions that nourish the brain little by little. When repeated over time, these daily habits become the architecture of a sharper mind. They strengthen the pathways the brain uses to store experiences, anchor thoughts, and recall information with confidence. Memory is not built in bursts. It is strengthened in the moments you return to something meaningful.

One of the most effective habits is reading. Reading engages attention in a way very few activities can. When you read, you ask your mind to follow a sequence, build images, hold ideas, and connect one paragraph to the next. Each sentence becomes a small exercise for working memory. Even reading for ten minutes a day can bring more clarity to your thinking because it trains your brain to stay with one idea for longer than the digital world usually allows. Reading aloud deepens this effect because it combines language, voice, and auditory processing. For children, hearing stories repeated again and again builds the foundation of lifelong recall. For adults, reading serves as mental nourishment that gently resets the mind from scattered thinking into focused engagement.

Play is another surprisingly powerful habit for memory. People often associate play with childhood, but the human brain responds to enjoyment throughout life. When you play a game that involves remembering patterns, predicting moves, or recalling what happened earlier, you activate neural circuits that support both long-term and working memory. Games like card matching, crossword puzzles, word associations, and strategy-based activities allow the brain to practise recall in a low-pressure environment. There is something freeing about learning through fun. The mind becomes more curious and attentive when joy is part of the process. Even small playful moments, like trying to remember a melody or mentally rehearsing a route before you walk, create invisible strengthening in the background.

Learning something new is one of the strongest habits for memory growth. When you attempt to learn a language, explore a musical instrument, or pick up a new skill, you do more than remember facts. You challenge your brain to create brand new neural pathways. This restructuring keeps the brain flexible and alert. Adults sometimes believe they have passed the age of learning new things, but in reality, the brain thrives on novelty. Even small commitments, like learning a few words in another language or practising a simple rhythm on a drum, activate cognitive processes that promote long-term memory resilience. The act of trying is what matters most. Each time you stretch your mind, you protect it from stagnation.

Cooking is another everyday activity that many people overlook as a memory exercise. Following a recipe involves sequencing, measuring, planning, and recalling steps in the correct order. When you cook a familiar dish from memory, you practise recall even more directly. The senses become involved, which strengthens memory by anchoring information in sight, smell, sound, and touch. Cooking offers the perfect blend of routine and creativity. Over time, you begin to remember ingredients without checking, and you intuitively recall what comes next. This builds confidence and creates a real-world example of memory functioning at its best: practical, embodied, and meaningful.

Names and faces are an area where many people struggle, and this struggle can be improved through simple everyday habits. When you meet someone, repeating their name aloud is a powerful way to tell your mind that the information matters. Paying focused attention during introductions prevents the name from slipping past the moment. Memory thrives on intention. If you choose to remember someone, the brain listens. Practising associations, whether visual or verbal, strengthens recall further. Over time, this becomes a natural part of how you engage socially, and the awkwardness of forgetting becomes far less common.

Repetition remains one of the oldest and most effective habits for strengthening memory. People sometimes resist repetition because it feels too obvious, yet the brain relies heavily on repeated exposure to encode information. Reciting something aloud, writing it down, or reviewing it later at night reinforces the neural connections that form memories. Even repeating daily tasks, such as placing your keys in the same spot or reviewing your schedule each morning, helps create a structured mental landscape that is easier to navigate. Memory loves familiarity and structure. When your life has rhythms, your recall becomes steadier.

Writing by hand is another habit with a surprising impact. In a digital world, typing has become the norm, but handwriting activates parts of the brain connected to attention and organisation. When you write a thought manually, you slow down enough for the information to embed itself more deeply. Journaling, planning your day, making notes, or recording reflections engages the mind in a way that strengthens recall and comprehension. There is something intimate about writing by hand. It turns memory into a physical act and gives thoughts a more permanent shape.

The most important truth about memory-friendly habits is that they do not demand perfection. They ask only for presence. When you read for pleasure, learn out of curiosity, play with ease, repeat what matters, speak names with intention, or write to organise your thoughts, you create a mental environment where memory can thrive. Small habits compound over time. The memory you want in your future is shaped by the actions you repeat today. Every moment of attention is a seed that grows into a sharper, more resilient mind.

ഊ

6

MEMORY FOR REAL-LIFE CHALLENGES

Memory becomes most meaningful when it helps us navigate real life. It is one thing to remember facts during study or enjoy a moment of nostalgia when a scent transports you back in time. It is something else entirely to recall the name of someone you have just met, to stay calm while retrieving information during an exam or presentation, or to hold onto the details of a conversation long after it is over. Memory is not only a cognitive ability. It is a social tool, an emotional anchor, and a guide that helps you move confidently through situations that matter. Understanding how memory behaves in real life makes you better equipped to use it purposefully rather than letting it slip away under pressure.

One of the most common real-world challenges is remembering names and faces. Many people assume they are simply bad with names, but in most cases, the problem is not ability. It is attention. When meeting someone new, the mind often hurries ahead to what you should say next or how you are presenting yourself. In that rush, the name barely gets registered. By slowing down during introductions and giving yourself a moment to focus, you tell your brain that the information matters. Repeating the name aloud strengthens the initial imprint, and noticing a distinctive feature creates an association that the mind can retrieve later. Over time, this gentle shift in awareness transforms social memory. Instead of fumbling for names, you remember them with ease, which builds trust, warmth, and a sense of connection in your interactions.

Academic or professional memory challenges are more structured but can feel far more intimidating. During exams, interviews, or presentations, people often experience a sudden mental blank that feels terrifying. This temporary disappearance of memory is usually caused by stress, not lack of preparation. When the body senses pressure, it shifts into survival mode. This tightens the mind and narrows access to stored information. The best way to overcome this is to practise retrieval even when you are not under pressure. Testing yourself regularly builds familiarity with the act of recalling information rather than only recognising it. That simple practice builds resilience. During an exam or presentation, the brain recognises the task, settles more quickly, and releases the information that is already stored. Deep breathing, grounding techniques, or taking a short pause also help. The mind often returns with the answer the moment the body relaxes.

Conversations are another area where memory plays a crucial yet unnoticed role. Being able to recall what someone said, how they said it, and how it made you feel determines the strength of your relationships. People feel valued when they realise you remember details they shared earlier. This kind of memory is strengthened through presence. When you listen with genuine attention rather than waiting for your turn to speak, your brain naturally retains more. Repeating details mentally after the conversation, reflecting on what you learned about the person, or making a note if the information is important, helps transform fleeting moments into lasting connections. Good memory in conversations is not a trick. It is a form of care.

Directional memory is a different kind of challenge. Some people navigate effortlessly, while others get disoriented easily. The difference often lies in how deeply you engage with your surroundings. When you rely entirely on GPS, the mind becomes passive and fails to build internal maps. When you pay attention to landmarks, street names, colours, and patterns, your brain begins to form a mental model of the area. This model becomes stronger each time you walk or drive the route without external guidance. A sense of direction is not an innate gift. It is a skill born from curiosity and mindful observation.

Emotional memory is one of the most powerful and complex forms of recall. While facts fade, emotional experiences remain vivid because they involve multiple regions of the brain. When you experience joy, disappointment, fear, or love, the memory imprints more deeply. This is why certain scents, songs, or places can bring back memories in an instant. Emotional memories can strengthen relationships, guide decisions, and help you understand who you are. But they can also become heavy when tied to pain or unresolved experiences. In such cases, memory protects you by hiding certain details until you are ready to process them. With support, reflection, and emotional safety, these memories often return in a gentler, more manageable form. This is not failure. It is resilience.

Real-life memory also includes the simple but frustrating lapses that happen during busy days. Forgetting where you placed your phone, losing track of your keys, or overlooking an appointment usually happens because the mind was occupied during the moment of action. These lapses can be reduced by returning to intention. When you place something down, say it to yourself or pause just long enough to notice it. When you finish a task, mentally mark it. These tiny acts of awareness strengthen everyday recall more than any complicated technique.

Memory in real life thrives when you bring attention to the present, practise retrieval regularly, and observe your surroundings with curiosity. It grows stronger when you slow down, listen deeply, and stay open to emotion. It is shaped not only by biology but by the way you move through the world. The challenges of remembering names, information, conversations, directions, and emotional experiences become easier when you understand the patterns beneath them. Memory is not only something you have. It is something you cultivate, one real-life moment at a time.

7

YOUR BRAIN

More Than a Memory Machine

Memory is often described as a mental function, something that happens in the brain as you move through your day. But the truth is much larger and more interconnected. Your brain does not store memories in isolation. It listens to your body, responds to your emotions, adapts to your internal chemistry, and depends deeply on the simplest rhythms of daily life. When the body is nourished, rested, balanced, and supported, memory thrives. When any part of that system is strained, even the strongest mind can feel foggy, forgetful, or overwhelmed. Understanding memory through the lens of the whole body allows you to protect it more wisely and strengthen it more easily.

The brain is one of the most energy-hungry organs you have. It consumes a significant portion of your daily nutrients to keep its neurons firing and its networks active. That is why nutrition is not merely helpful for memory but foundational to it. When the brain receives the vitamins, minerals, fats, and antioxidants it needs, it builds stronger connections between neurons, processes information more efficiently, and recovers more quickly from stress. Foods rich in Omega-3 fatty acids, folate, vitamin B12, magnesium, and antioxidants provide the raw material for sharper recall. Leafy greens, nuts, whole grains, fruits, and fish create an internal environment where memory can grow. In contrast, diets heavy in sugar, artificial preservatives, and processed foods create inflammation and slow cognitive speed. You may notice this as brain fog after a sugary snack or mental fatigue after a day of eating poorly. The science is clear and deeply practical. What you feed your body shapes how well your memory performs.

Sleep is equally powerful. A lack of sleep affects memory more quickly than almost any other factor. During rest, the brain sorts, organises, and strengthens the memories formed throughout the day. Without this nightly reset, information stays scattered, and the mind struggles to retrieve what it needs. This is why people who sleep poorly often experience moments of blankness, difficulty concentrating, or a sense that their thoughts are cloudy. Good sleep hygiene, consistent routines, and deep rest are not luxuries. They are essential tools for memory maintenance. Even short naps can revive the mind by giving it brief opportunities to process and reset. Understanding this helps you see sleep not as time taken from productivity but as the foundation that makes productivity possible.

Hormones also play a surprisingly large role in memory. They influence mood, clarity, focus, and the speed at which your brain processes information. The hormonal shifts that occur during menopause, pregnancy, adolescence, and midlife for both men and women can temporarily disrupt memory. These changes can bring forgetfulness, mental fog, and emotional fluctuations that make recall harder. Recognising this connection helps reduce panic or self-criticism during these phases. Instead of assuming something is wrong with your mind, you can support your body through gentle movement, good nutrition, hydration, and stress reduction. By understanding your internal chemistry, you make room for compassion and smarter care.

Hydration is another simple yet profound part of the memory puzzle. Even mild dehydration slows cognition and weakens recall. The brain is highly sensitive to fluid balance. When you go too long without water, the mind becomes tired and unfocused. This is why people often experience irritability, confusion, or forgetfulness on days when they have barely drunk anything. Keeping consistently hydrated is one of the easiest ways to support memory, yet one of the most commonly overlooked.

Movement is also connected to memory in more ways than most people realise. Physical activity increases blood flow to the brain, delivers oxygen to neurons, reduces stress hormones, and triggers the release of chemicals that support learning. Something as simple as a daily walk can noticeably improve mental clarity. Yoga, stretching, dancing, and swimming all contribute to a healthier brain ecosystem. The mind is not separate from the body. When you move, your brain wakes up. When your heart rate rises, your memory becomes more responsive.

The emotional environment you live in influences memory just as powerfully. Chronic stress, unresolved worries, and emotional overload can cloud recall and weaken attention. When your mind feels stretched thin, memory suffers because the brain is too busy trying to manage tension. Stress reduction techniques such as mindfulness, deep breathing, nature walks, or slow routines help the brain settle. A calm mind remembers more. Emotional regulation is not a psychological luxury. It is a memory tool.

All of these factors show that the brain is a living, breathing system that depends on harmony within the body. Memory is not just a mental skill that exists above the shoulders. It is the result of nourishment, rest, balance, movement, and emotional stability. When you take care of your body, you are also caring for your mind. When you choose to slow down, eat consciously, sleep deeply, and manage stress gently, you are choosing sharper recall and better cognitive resilience.

Understanding this body-mind connection changes how you approach your memory. Instead of chasing quick fixes or feeling frustrated by forgetfulness, you begin to see memory as something that can be cultivated through simple, sustainable habits. Every sip of water, every nourishing meal, every walk, every moment of rest becomes part of the larger work of supporting your brain. With this holistic approach, memory becomes more than a function. It becomes a reflection of how you live, how you care for yourself, and how you honour the relationship between your body and your mind.

8

NATURAL REMEDIES AND HERBAL SUPPORT

Throughout history, people have turned to plants, herbs, and natural remedies to strengthen the mind, improve alertness, and maintain clarity. Long before laboratory science emerged, ancient cultures observed which roots sharpened memory, which leaves calmed the mind, and which teas lifted a foggy sense of awareness. What is remarkable is that many of these traditions continue to be validated by modern research. Nature offers an entire library of gentle tools that support brain health, and while none of them can replace healthy habits or medical treatment where needed, they can play a meaningful role in keeping the brain energised and resilient.

Natural remedies work best when you approach them as part of a broader lifestyle. A herb cannot compensate for chronic stress or a lack of sleep, but it can complement a balanced routine. Many people turn to nature when they feel mentally tired or overwhelmed, not because they are seeking a miracle cure, but because they want a form of nourishment that feels grounded and sustainable. When used wisely, herbs and natural remedies offer precisely that. They support the nervous system, improve circulation, calm anxiety, and encourage the kind of steady mental energy that helps memory function consistently.

Many everyday spices found in kitchens across the world carry surprising cognitive benefits. Turmeric is one of the most studied spices for brain health. Its active compound, curcumin, has been linked to improved memory performance and reduced inflammation, particularly in older adults. It is not a fast-acting stimulant but a slow, steady supporter, and its effects build over weeks and months of consistent use. Fresh ginger offers a different kind of support. It promotes clear thinking and helps reduce mental sluggishness, partly due to compounds that improve blood flow. Cinnamon has been associated with heightened alertness and better processing speed. Even its aroma can lift your mood and sharpen your senses. These are small, familiar ingredients, yet when used regularly, they contribute to a clearer, more responsive mind.

Beyond culinary spices, certain herbs have long been valued for their ability to nourish cognitive function. Ginkgo biloba is one of the most widely researched herbal supplements in the world. It is believed to improve blood flow to the brain, support healthy neurons, and strengthen recall, particularly in older adults or those experiencing early cognitive fatigue. Consistency matters more than high dosage, and benefits tend to appear gradually. Gotu kola is valued for its soothing influence on the mind. People often use it to ease anxiety and support balanced energy, which indirectly aids memory by reducing mental tension. Siberian ginseng is a well-known adaptogen that helps the body cope with stress and maintain steady vitality throughout the day. Reducing the strain that chronic stress places on the brain helps preserve memory and focus.

Aromatherapy is another branch of natural support that many people find surprisingly effective. Certain scents activate the limbic system, which is closely tied to memory and emotional processing. Rosemary is one of the most well-known examples. Inhaling its scent during study or work sessions can increase alertness and strengthen recall. Basil can help calm mental restlessness and encourage clarity during overwhelming moments. Oils like peppermint and lemon awaken the senses, reduce fatigue, and create a fresher mental environment. These effects may sound subtle, but when used during daily routines, aromas can become powerful cues that prepare the brain for focus, relaxation, or recall. Something as simple as diffusing rosemary oil during a work session or keeping a small cotton pad with peppermint oil in your bag can become part of a helpful memory ritual.

It is important to remember that natural remedies work best in partnership with healthy habits. Herbs can strengthen memory, but they cannot override the effects of chronic stress, sleep deprivation, dehydration, or inadequate nutrition. If someone begins taking ginseng while skipping meals, or diffuses rosemary while staying up until dawn, the benefits will be minimal. Natural support works when the foundation is stable. A balanced diet, regular movement, proper hydration, and emotional steadiness create the environment in which herbs can do their best work.

At the same time, natural does not automatically mean risk-free. Different bodies respond differently to the same plants, and herbal supplements vary widely in quality across brands and regions. Some herbs can interfere with medications. Others may not be suitable during pregnancy or for individuals with certain health conditions. It is important to approach natural remedies with informed awareness. Consulting a qualified practitioner, understanding dosage, and choosing reputable sources are crucial steps. Paying attention to how your body responds, even after a few days of use, helps you understand what is actually working for you and what is not.

When approached thoughtfully, nature can become an ally in your journey toward sharper memory and clearer thinking. You might add turmeric to your meals each week, drink green tea in the afternoon instead of a sugary beverage, keep a rosemary diffuser on your desk, or explore herbal supplements under professional guidance. Each small choice becomes part of a larger pattern of care.

In many ways, natural remedies encourage a slower, more intentional relationship with yourself. Brewing a herbal tea, lighting a scented candle, or adding spices to your meals invites you to pause. These rituals are gentle reminders that memory thrives in a mind that is steady, rested, and nourished. The goal is not to chase heightened productivity but to restore balance so the mind can perform with ease.

Nature has always offered support to those who take the time to listen to it. One herb, one spice, one scent at a time, it invites you to nurture your mind with patience and awareness. When used consistently and wisely, natural remedies become more than tools. They become companions in your effort to cultivate a resilient, confident memory that grows stronger year after year.

ꙮ

9

CAFFEINE, SUPPLEMENTS, AND MODERN CONTROVERSIES

Caffeine has become one of the most common ways people try to sharpen their memory and stay mentally alert. It is woven into daily life so naturally that most of us do not even question its presence. A cup of tea before work, a quick coffee between tasks, an energy drink before a late study session, or a strong brew to push through an afternoon slump. Caffeine can indeed heighten awareness and improve reaction time, which is why so many depend on it during demanding periods. Yet it is also a substance that deserves respect, because the line between helpful stimulation and mental strain can become very thin. When used with intention and moderation, caffeine can support short-term mental focus. When used to mask chronic exhaustion, it can contribute to memory problems, anxiety, and disrupted sleep.

The way caffeine affects memory is complex. In the short term, it can help you stay alert enough to concentrate and can make information feel easier to grasp. Many people find that a small morning dose helps them start the day with a clearer mind. But caffeine does not improve memory directly. Instead, it creates a temporary feeling of wakefulness that can make learning more effective, especially when combined with good study habits. Problems arise when caffeine becomes a replacement for healthy routines such as enough sleep, proper nutrition, and structured mental breaks. Over time, relying on caffeine to stay awake can strain the nervous system, create energy crashes, worsen concentration, and disturb the deep sleep cycles that the brain depends on to consolidate memory.

Supplements are another area filled with confusion and marketing claims. The modern world offers an endless variety of powders, capsules, tonics, and drinks that promise sharper memory, instant focus, or improved brainpower. Some supplements have scientific support, while others rely more on appealing words than evidence. It is understandable that people want quick solutions, especially during periods of academic stress, demanding jobs, or memory changes related to ageing. The temptation to reach for the fastest option can be strong. But supplements are most effective when used as part of a balanced lifestyle rather than as shortcuts. The body responds best when nutrients from food, hydration, steady sleep, and emotional regulation are already in place. Supplements should refine a healthy routine, not replace it.

Some nutrients do have research supporting their cognitive benefits. Omega-3a three fatty acids, for example, play a significant role in brain health because they support cell structure and communication. Vitamin B complex supports energy metabolism and helps maintain healthy nerve function. Magnesium supports relaxation and can reduce tension that interferes with focused thinking. Antioxidants from berries, leafy greens, and certain vitamins help protect the brain from oxidative stress. These nutrients do not create dramatic changes overnight, but they help build a resilient foundation that allows memory to function smoothly. When deficiencies are present, targeted supplements can be very helpful. The key is to avoid guesswork. Blood tests, medical guidance, and professional evaluation provide the clarity needed to make informed decisions.

Despite the abundance of modern products, the supplement world has several controversies. One major concern is the quality and purity of products. Supplements are not all regulated with the same level of rigour, which means that dosages can vary, ingredients may be incomplete, and some formulas may contain fillers that reduce effectiveness. Another concern is that certain supplements interact with medications or existing health conditions. A product that is harmless for one person may be problematic for another. This is why professional guidance matters. The goal is not to avoid all supplements, but to choose them with careful awareness.

The cultural trend toward using quick-fix cognitive enhancers has also raised ethical and emotional questions. Many people turn to supplements or high caffeine intake because they feel pressured to perform at unrealistic levels. Students may feel the need to stay awake through long study nights. Professionals may push themselves to meet deadlines. Parents may struggle to balance multiple roles. In these situations, supplements may relieve the symptoms of a deeper imbalance without addressing the source. The pressure to always be alert, productive, and mentally sharp can create exhaustion that no product can fix. Memory thrives in a balanced life, not in a constantly overextended one.

A helpful way to navigate this landscape is to consider your intention before consuming any stimulant or supplement. Ask yourself whether you are supporting a healthy routine or trying to compensate for one that is draining you. Are you using caffeine to enhance your focus or to avoid dealing with chronic sleep loss? Are you taking supplements because of real need or because you feel obligated to keep up with modern expectations of productivity? These questions are not about judgment. They simply help you stay connected to your body's signals and choose what is genuinely supportive rather than reactive.

If you choose to use caffeine or supplements, there are practical ways to do so more safely. Small, consistent doses of caffeine often work better than large amounts that create rapid spikes and drops in energy. Pairing caffeine with proper hydration helps maintain balance. Allowing at least six hours between your last dose and bedtime protects your sleep cycle. When using supplements, follow evidence-based dosages, track how your body responds over several weeks, and use reputable sources. If something does not feel right, trust your intuition and adjust.

While modern culture often treats memory as something that can be hacked or boosted instantly, the truth is that memory thrives in environments of stability, nourishment, rest, and steady emotional regulation. Caffeine and supplements can support these conditions if used thoughtfully. They can also work against them if used in excess or with unrealistic expectations. Your brain is not a machine that responds instantly to a single substance. It is a living system that flourishes when your choices form a pattern of care rather than a cycle of quick fixes.

In the end, the most powerful memory strategy is a lifestyle that respects your mind's limits and strengths. When supplements or caffeine are used with awareness, they can become part of that lifestyle. When they are used as shortcuts, they only deepen the imbalance. The goal is to find a rhythm that lets your memory work with you, supported by thoughtful choices that honour your long-term well-being.

ജ്ജ

10

MEMORY AND LIFE TRANSITIONS

Memory is not a static skill that remains the same throughout our lifetime. It changes as we do. Every new season of life affects the mind in dramatic ways. Hormones shift, responsibilities increase, stress rises or settles, and the emotional weight of certain experiences deepens. Some transitions bring clarity and mental sharpness, while others create forgetfulness, fog, or confusion that feels out of character. Understanding these shifts is one of the most compassionate things you can do for yourself because it reminds you that changes in memory are not always signs of decline. They are often reflections of a life that is growing, moving, and adjusting to new realities.

Many people first notice memory challenges during periods of major stress or emotional upheaval. This can happen when starting a new job, caring for a newborn, moving to a new city, or coping with loss. Even positive change can create cognitive load. The mind becomes preoccupied with adapting to a new environment, managing unfamiliar responsibilities, or processing emotions that take up mental space. During these periods, memory may feel unreliable, but the real issue is often saturation. When the brain is juggling too many demands, it has less capacity to encode and recall information accurately. Instead of interpreting these lapses as failure, it helps to view them as signals that the mind is working very hard behind the scenes.

For many women, memory shifts become especially noticeable during pregnancy, postpartum recovery, and menopause. Hormones play a significant role in cognitive function, and fluctuations can affect recall, focus, and mental clarity. Pregnancy creates a unique mix of physical fatigue, emotional anticipation, and rapid hormonal change. Many expectant mothers experience what is often called pregnancy brain, a sense that details slip away easily or concentration feels harder to maintain. After childbirth, the mind often becomes consumed with the needs of the baby. Sleep becomes fragmented, routines are disrupted, and attention is constantly divided. This combination can make short-term memory feel scattered. These changes usually improve with time, rest, and stability, and they do not indicate long-term decline. They reflect the intensity of early parenthood.

Men experience cognitive shifts, too, although they are less widely discussed. Hormonal changes in middle adulthood can affect energy, stress tolerance, and mental clarity. These changes may not be dramatic, but they can influence memory indirectly by altering mood, sleep, or motivation. Men, like women, are deeply affected by life transitions such as career changes, caretaking responsibilities, ageing parents, or the pressure to maintain certain standards of success. Cognitive fog can emerge during times of internal pressure, even when it appears subtle on the outside. Memory often reflects the emotional burdens a person is carrying rather than their intellectual ability. Ageing introduces another layer of complexity. As people grow older, it is normal to notice shifts in how quickly information is retrieved. Words may take longer to recall. Multi-tasking may feel more demanding. Tasks that once felt automatic may require a bit more intention. These changes are not failures. They are reflections of a brain that has accumulated decades of experiences, responsibilities, and emotional history. What often declines with age is speed, not capability. In fact, older adults often show remarkable strengths in pattern recognition, emotional intelligence, long-term knowledge, and reflective decision-making. When supported with healthy habits, the ageing brain can remain vibrant and capable.

Life transitions also affect memory through changes in identity. When someone becomes a parent, retires, switches careers, ends a relationship, or starts a new chapter, their internal sense of self shifts. The mind adapts by reorganising priorities, values, and emotional anchors. This reorganisation can temporarily affect memory because the brain is sorting what matters most in a new context. Just as the body feels different after growth, the mind also rewires itself during major transitions. These rewiring periods may feel disorienting, but they often lead to greater mental resilience and emotional clarity once the adjustment settles.

What many people do not realise is that memory loss during transitions is often reversible. Once stress decreases, sleep improves, routines stabilise, and the emotional landscape becomes less turbulent, memory functions recover significantly. This is why the most helpful response is patience rather than panic. Supporting the body through nourishment, movement, quality rest, and emotional expression can restore mental clarity far more effectively than forcing productivity. The mind recovers best when it feels safe, supported, and understood.

It can be comforting to remember that memory is not purely a cognitive function. It is deeply connected to the body's rhythms, hormones, and emotional landscape. Each season of life brings its own cognitive signature. A person who feels forgetful during early parenthood may feel sharper years later. Someone who struggles with focus during a stressful career shift may find renewed clarity once they settle into a new role. Someone who experiences fog during menopause may regain stability with lifestyle adjustments. Memory is fluid. It heals, adapts, and evolves.

To navigate memory during life transitions with more ease, it helps to build small, supportive habits. Writing down important details reduces the pressure on your mind. Creating simple routines helps anchor your days. Choosing restorative activities such as walking, stretching, breathing exercises, or reflection gently stabilises mental clarity. Seeking support during emotionally heavy transitions helps unburden the mind. And reminding yourself that your cognitive ability is not defined by temporary fog can protect your confidence.

Life's transitions are not interruptions to your growth. They are part of it. Your memory will change across the years because your life changes. Every shift you experience leaves an imprint not only on your identity but also on your mind. When you meet these changes with understanding rather than fear, you create space for resilience to grow. You give your memory room to recover, recalibrate, and flourish in its own time. That is the real power of navigating transitions with awareness.

ഌ൫

11

SUPPORTING YOUR CHILD'S GROWING MEMORY

A child's memory is one of the most remarkable and delicate systems in human development. It is constantly growing, reorganising itself, and learning how to handle the world. Every experience, from a simple bedtime story to a difficult moment on the playground, becomes part of the internal library a child carries into adulthood. Children do not learn in the same way adults do. Their minds absorb in layers, relying heavily on repetition, emotional safety, sensory input, and the rhythms of daily life. Understanding how children form memories helps parents, teachers, and caregivers support them in a way that strengthens learning rather than overwhelming it.

Many parents worry when a child forgets instructions, misplaces toys, or seems unable to recall something taught the day before. In reality, this forgetfulness is not a failure. It is a sign that their memory systems are still under construction. Young children especially rely on external structure because their working memory is small and easily overloaded. They may focus deeply on one detail and lose sight of another. They may remember the colour of a balloon at a party but forget who handed it to them. Adults often misinterpret this selectiveness, but it reflects how a child's mind chooses what feels vivid, comforting, or emotionally important. When adults understand this, they can create environments that help memory form in a clearer, more organised way.

Children learn best when information is tied to emotion, movement, and repetition. A child may forget a math lesson but remember the tune of a song from a commercial because the song was fun, rhythmic, and repeated often. Emotion anchors memory, and this is true at every age, but especially in early childhood. This is why warm encouragement, patient explanations, and calm repetition create stronger learning than pressure or frustration. When a child feels safe, their mind opens. When they feel anxious, rushed, or criticised, their ability to remember drops sharply. Supporting memory is often less about drilling information and more about creating the emotional conditions where learning feels secure.

Routine is one of the most powerful tools for helping a child remember. Predictable daily rhythms act like bookmarks in the mind. When meals, sleep, study time, and play happen around the same time each day, the brain learns to anticipate what comes next. This anticipation strengthens memory circuits gradually and naturally. Even very small rituals help, such as reading before bed, reviewing schoolwork after a snack, or preparing the school bag every evening. These actions signal the brain to organise information instead of letting it float around without structure. Over time, routines build the mental scaffolding that allows children to handle more complex learning later.

Stories are another essential tool. Children remember stories far more easily than isolated facts because stories provide context, emotion, and meaning. Whether through books, personal anecdotes, or conversations, stories give children a way to connect information to real life. A story about a brave character helps a child remember what courage looks like. A story about a scientific discovery helps them recall how curiosity leads to answers. When parents and teachers use stories intentionally, they help children build mental anchors that support both learning and emotional development.

Movement also plays a vital role in memory formation. Children learn with their whole bodies. When they sing while clapping, write letters while tracing them in the air, or count blocks with their fingers, they are strengthening the connection between physical action and cognitive recall. Movement brings ideas to life. Even something as simple as taking a walk after studying can help older children consolidate what they learned that day. The brain thrives on rhythm and motion, especially in childhood, and movement often unlocks understanding in a way stillness cannot.

One of the most important things adults can do for a child's memory is to reduce unnecessary pressure. Children who fear making mistakes often remember less because their minds are focused on avoiding failure rather than understanding concepts. Encouragement helps far more than correction. When adults praise effort, progress, and resilience, they help strengthen the emotional foundation that supports long-term learning. When a child feels valued regardless of performance, they are more willing to take risks, ask questions, and explore ideas. These behaviours are essential for healthy memory development.

As children grow older, they begin to develop a sense of responsibility for their own learning. This transition is delicate. Parents can help by teaching simple memory tools in a gentle, encouraging way. These include practising retrieval rather than rereading, summarising lessons in their own words, visualising concepts with drawings, associating new ideas with familiar ones, and breaking tasks into smaller steps. These tools teach children how to work with their minds instead of fighting against them. The goal is not to create perfect recall, but to help children understand how to organise information in ways that feel natural.

Technology can support learning when used deliberately. Adults can help children use devices to reinforce memory by guiding them toward tools that encourage practice, creativity, and thoughtful exploration rather than endless passive consumption. Screens can overwhelm a child's memory when used without boundaries, but they can also enrich learning when they invite curiosity. The key is balance. When technology is paired with conversation, guidance, and human connection, it becomes a powerful partner in learning rather than a distraction from it.

Supporting a child's growing memory is ultimately about more than academics. It is about nurturing a sense of confidence, curiosity, and emotional security that will carry them through life. Every child deserves to learn in an environment where questions are welcomed, mistakes are part of the process, and growth happens at a pace that respects their unique rhythm. When adults understand how children internalise their world, they can guide them with greater patience and clarity. They can help them build mental tools that strengthen not only their memory but also their identity, their resilience, and their sense of competence.

A child's memory is a living system that grows through warmth, repetition, creativity, and trust. When nurtured with care, it becomes a powerful foundation for lifelong learning. When protected from unnecessary pressure, it becomes a place where confidence can flourish. And when supported through stories, movement, routines, and patient guidance, it becomes a source of strength that shapes the entire arc of a child's development.

ᘓᘐ

12

REMEMBERING NAMES, FACES, AND PEOPLE

Remembering people is one of the most meaningful forms of memory we possess, yet it is also one of the most fragile. Names slip away during introductions, faces blend together in crowded rooms, and even familiar people sometimes feel strangely distant when our minds are overloaded. Social memory is not simply about recalling information. It is about connection, empathy, and the way our brain prioritises human relationships. In an age where conversations are interrupted by notifications and interactions are scattered across digital platforms, remembering people has become more challenging than ever. But it remains deeply important because the ability to remember someone communicates value, attention, and respect. It tells the other person that they matter.

Most people assume they are bad at remembering names, but the truth is usually much simpler. When someone introduces themselves, we often hear the sound of their name, but we do not store it because our attention is divided. We may be thinking about how we look, how to respond, or what we should say next. Our mind shifts into self-preservation mode rather than listening carefully. The moment passes, and the name vanishes as if it were never spoken. This is not poor memory. It is simply a lapse in presence. When we slow down, look directly at the person, and allow the name to register with genuine intention, the brain begins to record it more clearly.

Faces are another form of memory that depends heavily on attention. The human brain is naturally wired to recognise faces, and certain regions of the brain are dedicated entirely to this task. Yet modern life pulls our focus toward screens far more than toward human expressions. We may glance at people rather than truly observe them. We may notice features but not patterns, and without a pattern, the brain struggles to file these impressions in a stable way. Remembering a face requires the same ingredients as recalling anything else. We need interest, awareness, emotional relevance, and a moment of recognition. When we give someone even a few seconds of full attention, we create a mental snapshot that is far harder to forget.

It helps to understand that remembering people is deeply tied to emotion and meaning. The mind holds on to what feels important. If a person reminds us of someone else, stands out through warmth or humour, or shares a story that sparks emotion, their name and face are much easier to recall. This is why small details matter. If we notice a person's tone, their choice of words, the way they gesture, or a small fact they reveal about themselves, these details act as memory anchors. They turn a fleeting interaction into something our brain can store. When we link a name to a distinctive feature, a piece of information, or a conversation moment, the memory strengthens naturally.

Many people forget names because they are trying to remember the name itself instead of creating context. Names are abstract. They only become meaningful when we attach them to something vivid. If someone says, "My name is Arjun," and we simply repeat the word silently, we may still forget it moments later. But if we connect that name to something personal, such as "Arjun loves trekking" or "Arjun has a warm smile," the mind now has a place to file it. The goal is not to memorise mechanically, but to create meaning through attention and association.

This is especially important in a world where social contact is scattered, brief, and constantly shifting. Digital life encourages rapid interaction. We scroll through faces, skim through comments, and glance at profile pictures without any real depth. These habits weaken the brain's ability to notice people fully. To strengthen memory, we must reverse the pattern by bringing more presence into our social encounters. When meeting someone in person, slowing down for a few extra moments can make a dramatic difference. When connecting online, taking a moment to read someone's message carefully or view their picture with intention can help the brain form clearer impressions.

Perhaps the greatest challenge is juggling the emotional demands of remembering many people at once. We meet colleagues, acquaintances, neighbours, clients, and extended family members regularly. Each connection carries different expectations, and the brain can feel overloaded. Instead of pressuring yourself to remember everyone perfectly, it helps to focus on clarity over quantity. When you choose to connect more deliberately with a few people at a time, your memory becomes stronger. Over time, these small choices reinforce the neural pathways involved in social recognition.

There are practical ways to support this process without breaking the reflective flow of your interactions. You can practice gentle techniques such as repeating the person's name naturally in conversation, silently visualising their face for a few seconds after you meet them, or linking their name to an image or emotion. You can notice one distinct feature, such as the way they laugh or the way their eyes brighten when they speak about something meaningful. You can ask a simple question that invites them to share something personal, because stories are easier to remember than isolated facts. You can also review your day in the evening and mentally walk through the people you interacted with. This small reflection strengthens recall and slowly builds long-term memory.

Children and adolescents learn social memory differently from adults, and they often benefit from explicit guidance. A child may forget a classmate's name but remember the colour of their water bottle. This is normal because their memory is still developing and tends to prioritise sensory details. Gently helping them link names to actions, feelings, or activities can make a big difference. Adolescents, on the other hand, may remember faces effortlessly but struggle with names because they are preoccupied with social belonging and self-image. Encouraging them to be present in conversations and to notice people beyond surface impressions teaches them the emotional value of attention.

At every age, the ability to remember people is a form of care. When you recall someone's name, their story, or even a small detail they shared, you communicate respect. You show them that what they said mattered to you. This strengthens relationships and builds trust. It makes social interactions warmer and more grounded. Remembering people is not simply a cognitive skill but a deeply human one. It shapes how we bond, how we build community, and how we create emotional safety.

In a rapidly moving world, taking the time to truly see people is becoming rare. Yet it is this very act of seeing that strengthens memory most powerfully. When we meet someone with intention, listen with focus, and observe with curiosity, we give our mind the space it needs to remember naturally. Social memory grows when presence is present. It grows when we care enough to slow down. It grows when we choose connection over distraction, and when we value people not as fleeting encounters but as meaningful experiences.

ꙮ

13

MOVEMENT AND MEMORY

When we think of memory, we often picture the brain as a separate universe, organising thoughts, storing experiences, and retrieving information. It feels like a mental world that lives apart from the physical body. Yet memory is not an isolated cognitive function. It is deeply connected to how we move, breathe, and inhabit our bodies. Our muscles, heart, lungs, and even the simple sway of our posture influence how well we remember. The relationship between movement and memory is intimate and often underestimated. Every step we take, every stretch we perform, and every moment we allow the body to awaken with energy is a message to the brain. It says, "I am alive, and I am paying attention."

The human brain evolved in motion. Our ancestors survived by walking, running, searching, climbing, and navigating constantly shifting terrain. The brain learned to remember because it needed to. It needed to recall where food grew, which paths were safe, and which dangers to avoid. Movement sharpened awareness, and awareness strengthened memory. When the body was active, the brain became alert and responsive. Although our world has changed drastically, this biological truth remains. When we move, the mind becomes clearer. When the body is still for too long, our thoughts become sluggish and unfocused. Memory thrives on physical engagement, and it suffers when the body is ignored.

Modern life has made stillness the default. We sit through long meetings, long commutes, and long hours behind screens. Even leisure has become sedentary. This stillness is not rest. It is stagnation. Over time, the body sends signals of fatigue, the mind grows dull, and memory becomes harder to access. The brain depends on oxygen, circulation, and the gentle stimulation that movement provides. Without these, the neural pathways responsible for memory begin to slow. It becomes harder to learn new things, harder to recall details, and harder to concentrate. Many people mistakenly believe they are losing their memory when, in reality, their bodies are simply under-stimulated.

Movement nourishes the brain by increasing blood flow, which delivers oxygen and nutrients that support cognitive processes. When you engage in physical activity, your heart pumps more vigorously, and your breathing deepens. This creates a fresh supply of energy that travels directly to the brain, helping you think more clearly. It is not surprising that many people say they remember things better after a walk or find solutions while pacing around a room. Physical activity activates regions of the brain involved in planning, problem-solving, and memory formation. It is as if movement gently shakes sleeping thoughts awake and invites clarity to return.

There is also a psychological dimension to this connection. Movement shifts your emotional state, and your emotional state influences how well you remember. When you feel anxious or weighed down, your mind narrows and becomes preoccupied with worry. It becomes difficult to store new information because the brain is busy trying to protect you from perceived threats. Movement, especially rhythmic motion like walking, swimming, or gentle dancing, allows the mind to soften. It loosens tension, opens mental space, and creates a sense of calm that supports memory retention. Even small movements, such as stretching your neck, rolling your shoulders, or breathing deeply, can change the emotional environment within your mind.

Not all movement needs to be intense. Memory thrives on consistency more than effort. A simple daily walk can be more powerful than a high-intensity workout performed occasionally. What matters is the repetition, the rhythm, and the message you send your brain when you choose to move. Daily activity teaches your mind that you are engaging with life. It reinforces clarity, attentive presence, and emotional stability. Over time, these small acts accumulate and create resilience in your memory. Many people underestimate how much their cognitive function improves when they adopt even modest movement habits.

Certain types of movement bring unique benefits to memory. Activities that require coordination, such as yoga, martial arts, dance, or ball sports, create stronger neural connections because they challenge both the body and the mind. These activities ask you to remember sequences, maintain balance, and respond to changing conditions. They stimulate the hippocampus, the part of the brain heavily involved in memory formation. Even simple coordination exercises like tapping different rhythms or balancing on one leg can activate neural circuits that sharpen recall.

Outdoor movement creates another layer of benefit. Natural environments have been shown to reduce stress and restore cognitive energy. When you walk through a park, listen to rustling leaves, or feel sunlight on your skin, the brain receives sensory input that nurtures attention and memory. Nature acts as a gentle reset, helping your mind recover from the constant stimulation of modern life. This recovery strengthens working memory, which is essential for learning, problem-solving, and decision-making. People often report that ideas flow more easily when they are outside, and this is not imagination. It is the brain responding to a healthier environment.

Movement also influences long-term brain health. Research has consistently shown that regular physical activity reduces the risk of memory-related conditions that appear later in life. It supports the growth of new neurons, strengthens existing networks, and protects the brain from inflammation. While no one can control every aspect of ageing, movement offers a powerful way to preserve memory as the years pass. It becomes a promise you make to your future self. The steps you take today create the clarity you will carry tomorrow.

Sometimes the simplest movements are the most meaningful. Standing up from your chair every hour, stretching your arms toward the ceiling, rotating your ankles, or taking a slow walk after a meal can anchor the mind in a state of renewed focus. These small choices remind your brain that you are present, engaged, and attentive. They create moments of restoration throughout your day, each one strengthening the foundation of memory.

To truly benefit from movement, it helps to view it not as an obligation, but as a companion to your mind. When you move, you are creating space inside yourself for clarity. You are telling your memory, "I am willing to support you. I am willing to show up." This intention changes the way movement feels. It becomes less about physical fitness and more about cognitive care. Even those who believe they dislike exercise often find comfort in gentle activities like walking slowly, stretching on the floor, or breathing in sync with a calm rhythm. Movement becomes a conversation between the body and the brain, and this conversation leads to improved memory.

As you explore the connection between movement and memory, you may find that your mind becomes more aware of your body. You may notice tension in your shoulders or heaviness in your breath. You may sense urges to stand, walk, release, or shift your posture. These signals are your body's way of guiding you toward mental clarity. Listening to them strengthens the cooperation between body and mind, and this cooperation builds a healthier memory system.

Memory does not exist in isolation. It is sustained by the flow of life that moves through you. When your body is active, your mind remains agile. When your body becomes stagnant, your memory begins to fade. True cognitive strength is built through movement that nurtures your entire being. Whether you choose to walk, dance, stretch, swim, or simply breathe deeply, the important thing is that you move with intention. Movement is a form of companionship and care that supports the longevity, clarity, and vibrancy of your memory.

ꙮ

14

MEMORY AND SCIENTIFIC RESEARCH

Memory is one of the mind's greatest mysteries. For centuries, poets and philosophers tried to describe it, and physicians attempted to understand it, yet it remained an elusive presence. We know what memory feels like, but grasping how it truly works has always been a challenge. Only in recent decades has science begun to illuminate what lies beneath our recollections. With modern tools, researchers can observe the brain as it learns, remembers, and forgets. With each discovery, our understanding of memory deepens, revealing a world far more intricate and hopeful than imagined.

Scientific research shows that memory is not a single function. It is a network of interconnected processes, each shaped by experience, environment, and biology. It is both delicate and resilient. It changes as we age and adapts with each new demand placed upon it. Memory results from thousands of small actions within the brain, from chemical signals to electrical pulses to the growth of new neurons. These actions are invisible to us, yet they are responsible for some of our most cherished experiences.

The centres of memory are not scattered randomly. They sit in regions of the brain such as the hippocampus and the entorhinal cortex. These areas store the stories of our lives and help us make sense of the world. Researchers now understand that these regions are often the first to change during memory-related conditions. When the hippocampus begins to lose its capacity, the ability to form new memories begins to fade. This is why some conditions begin with short-term forgetfulness before affecting older memories. The brain holds onto the past until the present becomes too difficult to manage.

For many years, people believed the brain could not regenerate. They were taught that once neurons died, they could never be replaced. This idea created fear, especially among older adults who worried that memory loss was inevitable. But modern research has transformed this narrative. Scientists have discovered that the adult brain can create new neurons through a process called neurogenesis. This discovery opened a door to hope. It revealed that memory is not frozen. It is alive and capable of repair. The brain constantly rewires itself and adapts to new experiences. When we learn, move, or challenge ourselves, new pathways form. Even damaged regions sometimes find alternate routes to preserve our ability to remember.

This new understanding has inspired countless studies. Researchers now explore how habits, diet, movement, and emotional well-being influence neurogenesis. They have found that physical exercise encourages the growth of new brain cells. They have found that stress slows down neural regeneration. They have found that learning new skills strengthens the connections between neurons. Every small action we take affects the inner landscape of our minds. This means that memory can often be supported long before serious decline appears.

Scientific research has also explored the role of nutrition. Omega-3 fats, green tea, berries, and B vitamins are not just healthy additions to our plates. They support the chemical environment that memory relies on. They reduce inflammation, supply antioxidants, and provide the building blocks the brain needs to function. Studies have shown that people who consume nutrient-rich foods consistently perform better on memory tests than those who rely on processed diets. This reinforces what many traditional cultures have always believed: food has a profound impact on mental clarity.

One of the most extensive areas of research focuses on age-related conditions such as Alzheimer's disease. Although a cure does not yet exist, there is more knowledge and more direction than ever before. Researchers have discovered genetic factors that influence risk. They have explored how inflammation affects the brain. They have found that early lifestyle habits play a major role in determining long-term cognitive health. Some studies reveal that long-term physical activity delays the progression of memory loss. Others show that social interaction protects the brain by creating cognitive reserves that help compensate for early damage. These findings show that even when challenges arise, the brain works hard to preserve itself.

Experimental therapies are also emerging. Scientists are studying how light stimulation may help reactivate memory circuits. Some researchers explore how sound frequencies can improve clarity and mood. Others are investigating how virtual reality can help preserve cognitive skills by immersing individuals in environments that challenge memory, movement, and attention simultaneously. These technologies are still in their early stages, but they show how future memory support may look very different from today's approaches.

Alongside these innovations, researchers continue to study the effects of sleep. Sleep remains one of the most powerful tools for memory. During deep rest, the brain processes events, clears waste, and stores information. When sleep is disrupted, memory becomes unstable. When sleep is restored, it strengthens again. This connection has inspired studies into sleep therapy, sleep hygiene, and sleep patterns that best support cognitive health. These findings demonstrate that something as ordinary as rest is one of the most profound memory protectors we have.

Another emerging area of research examines how technology affects memory. Researchers observe how constant notifications, multitasking, and digital overstimulation overload the working memory system. They explore how too much screen exposure shortens attention span and affects the brain's ability to store information effectively. These insights are shaping conversations about digital wellbeing and leading to practical recommendations for healthier technology use. The goal is not to eliminate devices, but to use them in ways that support mental clarity rather than diminish it.

Despite all these advances, the most encouraging message from memory research is simple. The future of memory health is not only in the hands of scientists. It is in the hands of everyday individuals. Many of the strongest protective factors are accessible to anyone. Movement, nutrition, learning, rest, emotional balance, and meaningful relationships all shape the brain. They influence neuron growth, strengthen connections, and support resilience. Research confirms what life has always shown. A balanced life is a powerful foundation for a healthy mind.

The study of memory continues to evolve. New discoveries appear each year, and each one brings fresh possibilities. Yet amid the excitement of modern science, one truth remains timeless. Memory flourishes when we nurture ourselves. It grows when we care for our minds and bodies, when we stay curious, and when we stay connected. Science can guide us, but we shape our own mental landscape through the choices we make each day.

15

THE STUDY OF MEMORY IMPROVEMENT

The study of memory improvement begins with a simple truth. Memory is not fixed. It is not a rigid structure that slowly wears out with age. It is a living, adapting system shaped by what we do, what we feel, how we move, and how we learn. Scientists, psychologists, teachers, and even philosophers have spent centuries exploring how memory can be strengthened. With every generation, the understanding becomes clearer. Improvement is possible at almost any age, and often easier than people believe.

Modern research shows that memory thrives when the brain is used in meaningful ways. The mind sharpens through challenge, repetition, and emotional engagement. These principles appear across cultures and across time. The techniques may differ, but the core idea remains constant. When we use the mind purposefully, it grows. When we avoid mental challenges, it softens. This responsiveness is possible because of a remarkable ability known as neuroplasticity.

Neuroplasticity refers to the brain's capacity to reorganise itself, to grow new connections, and to adapt to new experiences. Each time we learn something new, the brain subtly rewires itself. Each time we practice a skill, the pathway becomes stronger. Each time we repeat a meaningful action, neurons fire in synchrony and build a durable network that supports future recall.

This truth has guided researchers to explore the conditions that make learning easier and the habits that help memory flourish. One of the earliest insights came from observing animals. Studies with mice navigating mazes revealed that memory improves through structured challenge. When the maze became more complex, the mice learned faster and remembered more because their brains were forced to adapt. Their pathways grew stronger with practice and repetition. Similar patterns appear in studies of birds that migrate thousands of kilometres using environmental memory, or dogs that learn commands and sequences, or parrots that recall melodies and spoken words. These examples suggest that memory improvement follows universal rules. Challenge supports growth. Repetition strengthens skill. Emotional relevance deepens retention.

Human memory research adds another layer to this understanding. People do not only remember facts. They remember experiences, meanings, and emotions. This is why teaching strengthens memory. When someone explains a concept to another person, they must organise the idea, simplify it in their own words, and present it with clarity. This process anchors the information more deeply than silent reading ever could. The same principle appears in storytelling. When we turn memories into narratives, they become anchored in structure and emotion, making them easier to recall and harder to lose.

Scientists have also studied how habits influence memory. People with strong routines often remember more because consistent patterns reduce cognitive strain. When part of life follows predictable rhythms, the brain has more capacity for new information. Simple habits such as organising spaces, keeping items in consistent locations, reviewing information at set times, or using cues like music or scents can dramatically improve memory performance. These habits do not replace memory. They support it. They create an environment in which recall becomes natural rather than stressful.

Some of the most promising research explores how different styles of learning influence memory. Visual learners often remember best through imagery and colour. Auditory learners recall through sound, rhythm, or spoken repetition. Kinesthetic learners absorb information through movement and hands-on activity. When people match their study method to their natural learning style, memorisation becomes easier and more enjoyable. This is why children remember songs long before they remember written text and why adults often recall dance steps or recipes learned through physical repetition.

Memory improvement also benefits from a state often overlooked. Joy. The mind remembers more when it is emotionally engaged. Learning a new hobby, revisiting a childhood interest, participating in a lively conversation, or reading a book that sparks curiosity all enhance recall because they make learning meaningful. The brain treats enjoyment as a cue to preserve the moment. This is why boredom weakens memory and why excitement strengthens it. Emotional connection creates stronger neural pathways than information delivered without feeling.

Researchers also emphasise the role of reflection. When people pause at the end of a day and mentally review what they learned, whom they met, what they read, and what they want to remember, they reinforce memory consolidation. This practice mirrors systems used by memory champions who mentally revisit information before sleep to strengthen the neural imprint. Even a few minutes of mindful review can make the difference between remembering for a day and remembering for a lifetime.

Technology has inspired another branch of memory research. Tools like virtual reality simulations, neurofeedback devices, and digital memory trainers show promise in helping individuals engage their minds in more immersive ways. These tools create environments that activate multiple senses at once, a powerful combination for memory retention. While still developing, these innovations reflect a future where cognitive training may become more personalised, interactive, and accessible.

Yet with all these breakthroughs, the most powerful discoveries remain beautifully simple. Memory improves when life is enriched with learning, movement, routine, and curiosity. It improves when stress is managed and sleep is respected. It improves when we engage with others, tell stories, share knowledge, and experience new activities. Modern research and ancient wisdom converge on the same message. Memory grows when we use it. It weakens when we neglect it. Improvement is not the result of a single grand technique but a collection of small, sustainable practices that build strength over time.

The study of memory improvement continues to grow, offering new tools, new hope, and new possibilities. But the essence remains unchanged. Memory is not a burden to fear. It is a companion that grows with you. As you challenge your mind, feed it well, give it rest, and approach life with curiosity, your memory becomes clearer, stronger, and more resilient. The path to improvement is not complicated. It begins with awareness. It continues with consistency. And it flourishes when you decide to engage with your mind as an active, evolving part of your life.

ꕥ

16

DESIGN YOUR PERSONAL MEMORY PLAN

Creating a personal memory plan is one of the most powerful steps you can take toward strengthening your mind. Memory thrives on intention. It responds to consistent care, meaningful habits, and a genuine desire to grow mentally sharper. This chapter brings together everything you have learned throughout the book and turns it into a clear, yet flexible plan that you can adapt to your own lifestyle. A good memory plan does not require perfection or intensity. It requires steadiness, awareness, and small steps that accumulate into lasting transformation.

Before shaping your plan, take a moment to reflect on why you want to improve your memory. Your purpose will guide your progress. Some people want to remember names better because it improves relationships. Others hope to stay mentally sharp as they grow older. Students want better recall for exams. Parents want to help children strengthen their learning. Older adults want to stay confident and independent. Whatever your reason, acknowledge it gently. When intentions are clear, habits grow with far more ease.

A powerful memory plan begins by understanding what you want to improve. Memory is not one skill. It is a combination of many abilities. Short-term recall, long-term storage, focus, emotional memory, spatial memory, and everyday functional memory all play different roles. When you know what matters most to you, you can build habits that support those specific areas. Someone who struggles with misplacing items often benefits from environmental organisation and deliberate placement. Someone who struggles with names benefits from repetition and visual association. Someone who wants overall cognitive health benefits from movement, nutrition, sleep, and regular mental challenge.

The next step is choosing practices that strengthen memory gently and consistently. The best memory plans weave together physical, mental, emotional, and environmental strategies because memory itself relies on all these dimensions. Rather than trying to do everything at once, begin by choosing a few habits that feel natural to you. Consistency matters far more than quantity. Even one small habit practised daily can create powerful changes in memory.

Here are some categories to guide your selection. You do not need them all. Choose what speaks to your lifestyle and your goals.

Daily Mental Nourishment

Memory strengthens with use, so giving your mind meaningful stimulation each day is one of the core pillars of improvement. Reading for fifteen minutes, learning a new word, practising a language, solving a puzzle, or reviewing what you learned during the day all build stronger recall. What matters most is that the activity engages your attention in a focused and enjoyable way. When the mind enjoys learning, it remembers with less effort and more clarity.

Physical Movement as Mental Fuel

Movement nourishes the brain with oxygen, stimulates neuron growth, and reduces stress. Including gentle exercise in your daily routine is one of the simplest and most effective ways to support long-term memory. A twenty-minute walk, stretching in the morning, dancing to music, or swimming occasionally all promote cognitive health. You do not need intense workouts. You need movement that feels natural, pleasant, and consistent. When the body is active, the mind becomes more receptive, focused, and alert.

Nutrition and Hydration

Food shapes memory in ways we often overlook. A diet rich in greens, nuts, whole grains, fruits, berries, and Omega-3 sources gives the brain the nutrients it needs to maintain strong neural pathways. Hydration is equally important because even mild dehydration can create brain fog. A memory plan should include mindful eating rather than rules. Small changes such as drinking water throughout the day, adding one serving of vegetables to a meal, or choosing fruit over sugary snacks can make a significant difference.

Intentional Memory Techniques

Memory tools like mnemonics, repetition, mental stories, or visual association are essential parts of your plan if your goal is to recall specific information more reliably. These techniques turn memory into an active process rather than a passive expectation. They can be used for remembering names, studying for exams, recalling daily tasks, or preparing presentations. With time, these techniques become second nature, and your confidence in recall grows.

Environmental Support

Your surroundings influence your memory far more than you might think. A cluttered environment creates mental friction and makes recall harder. An organised space with designated places for frequently used items gives the mind relaxed clarity. Simple systems such as placing keys in the same location, keeping a visible calendar, or using a notebook for daily reminders strengthen practical memory. The environment is a silent partner in mental performance. When your space is clear, your mind becomes clearer too.

Emotional and Psychological Balance

Stress, worry, and emotional overload are some of the most powerful disruptors of memory. A personal memory plan must include strategies that help you stay emotionally centred. This may be journaling, meditation, long walks, moments without screens, practising gratitude, or spending time with people who bring you peace. When the mind feels safe and supported, memory improves naturally. Emotional wellness is not a luxury. It is a foundation for cognitive clarity.

Once your habits are chosen, the next step is building them into a rhythm. A memory plan works best when it blends into your life rather than feels like a heavy obligation. You might choose a morning walk, an afternoon reading ritual, or a nightly review of your day. You might place reminders around your home or set gentle alarms. You might pair habits together, such as stretching while listening to an audiobook or reviewing notes while drinking tea. The more you integrate the habits into your normal routine, the easier they become to maintain.

Tracking progress can also deepen your improvement. A simple journal can help you notice what works, what feels effortless, and what needs adjustment. You may realise that you recall names better after repeating them aloud, or that you think more clearly on days when you take morning walks. You may find that hydration helps your mental clarity or that evening reflection strengthens long-term retention. These observations guide you toward a plan that truly fits your natural rhythm.

Above all, remember that memory improves with patience. Some days you will feel sharper than others. Some habits will take time to feel natural. The goal is not to become perfect. The goal is to become aware, consistent, and compassionate with yourself. Memory grows gently when nurtured. Every small effort accumulates. Every moment of attention strengthens the mind. Every new habit becomes a seed for cognitive resilience.

Your memory plan is not a rigid system. It is a living guide that grows with you. It adapts as your needs change. It responds to your energy, your goals, and your season of life. When approached with intention and kindness, it becomes a powerful roadmap for lifelong mental strength, sharper recall, and a more confident sense of self.

CONCLUSION

As you reach the end of this book, pause for a moment and recognise how much you have already learned about your own mind. Memory is not a single skill. It is a living tapestry woven from your habits, your emotions, your biology, your routines, your relationships, and the way you move through the world each day. It is both delicate and resilient, influenced by small actions and shaped by choices that often feel ordinary in the moment. Yet those choices slowly become the foundation of your mental clarity, your confidence, and your sense of self.

Memory is not meant to be flawless. Forgetting is part of being human. It gives the mind space to grow, adapt, and absorb new knowledge. What matters most is not perfection but awareness. Every time you take care of your body, your emotions, or your daily routines, you support your memory. Every time you sleep well, nourish yourself with intention, challenge your mind, or allow it to rest, you strengthen the mental pathways that help you remember who you are and what you value.

As you have discovered, memory is not separate from life. It is deeply connected to how you live each day. A calm morning, a thoughtful conversation, a short walk, a moment of laughter, a nutritious meal, or a mindful pause all shape the brain in lasting ways. The mind is always listening. It listens to your habits, your stress levels, your joy, your learning, your relationships, and even the moments when nothing much seems to be happening. In these simple experiences, memory finds its rhythm.

If your memory has felt weak or unreliable in the past, let this book remind you that change is possible at every age. The brain responds to care, nourishment, repetition, rest, and new experiences. It responds to music, movement, sunlight, creativity, connection, and curiosity. It responds to self-compassion, especially during periods of stress or change. You are never stuck with the mind you have today. It is always capable of strengthening, reorganising, and growing in new directions.

Improving memory is not about turning yourself into a machine that never forgets. It is about building a mind that feels supported, energised, and able to serve you in the moments that matter. It is about remembering names because you value your relationships. It is about recalling information with confidence because you trust your ability to learn. It is about staying mentally steady through life's transitions and emerging with clarity rather than confusion. It is about staying connected to yourself so that your memories enrich your life instead of slipping away unnoticed.

This journey is ongoing. Some days you will feel mentally sharp. Other days will feel cloudy. This is natural. It is not a sign of failure but a reminder to return to the gentle practices that support your mind. A short walk. A glass of water. A moment of slow breathing. A night of healthy sleep. A page from a book. A conversation that brings warmth. Small actions create large changes when done with intention and consistency.

As you step forward, carry this truth with you. Your memory is not a fixed capacity but a lifelong companion that grows when nurtured. It reflects how you treat yourself. It strengthens with care. It heals with time. It flourishes with curiosity. And it becomes more resilient each time you choose practices that honour both your mind and your body.

You do not need dramatic changes to keep your mind strong. You need small, steady commitments that feel natural to you. Every good choice acts as a vote in favour of your future clarity. Every act of self-kindness protects the part of you that remembers. Every moment spent learning or reflecting anchors your identity in deeper ways.

Your memory is your story. It carries your joys, your lessons, your mistakes, your relationships, your experiences, and your hopes for the future. It is one of the most precious aspects of your life because it connects all the moments that make you who you are. Nourish it with care. Strengthen it with intention. Trust that it can grow.

And remember this above all: you are capable of far more than you realise. Your mind is adaptable, generous, and ready to support you. With patience, consistency, and compassion, you can continue to build a memory that stays steady, confident, and deeply alive for many years to come.

ᘓᘐ